Giovani dos Santos

To the Top!

2012 Returns once again to Tottenham Hotspur; helps Mexican team win Olympic gold medal.

2011 Giovani Dos Santos is sent on loan to Racing Santander on January 31.

Participates in the Gold Cup and helps to defeat the United States team on June 25.

2010 Giovani is loaned out to Galatasaray in the Turkish Super League.

2009 Transferred to Ipswich Town, on March 13.

Summoned to play at the CONCACAF tournament, where Mexico becomes champion.

2008 Transferred to Tottenham Hospur on June 4.

2007 Debuts with the senior team of Mexico on September 9.

2006 Debuts officially with FC Barcelona on July 28.

2005 Wins the Silver Ball in the U-17 World Cup. Mexico wins the championship.

2002 Giovani hired to play with the youth divisions of Barcelona.

2001 Participates with the youth divisions of CF Monterrey in the U-12 World Cup in France, and ends as scoring champion.

1995 Plays for the first time in a kids club at the age of 6.

1989 Giovani Dos Santos is born in Mexico City on May 1.

Personal File

Name: Giovani Dos Santos Ramírez

Nickname: Gio

Birthplace: Mexico City

Nationality: Mexican

Zodiacal sign: Taurus

Height: 5 feet 8.5 inches (1.74 m)

Twitter: @giovani_oficial

Position: Forward

Number with Tottenham: 17

Matches: 79

Record: 17 goals

Matches for Mexico: 59

International goals for Mexico: 14

ISBN-13: 978-1-4222-2650-6 (hc) — 978-1-4222-9191-7 (ebook)

Printing (last digit) 9 8 7 6 5 4 3 2 1
Printed and bound in the United States of America.
CPSIA Compliance Information: Batch #S2013. For further
information, contact Mason Crest at 1-866-MCP-Book.

About the Author: Ana Patricia Valay is a Mexican television and radio journalist committed to the truth and social journalism. She also writes reports for print media and has a radio show online, which is transmitted from San Diego to a worldwide audience. Her concerns are oriented to inform, guide and promote citizen participation for the sake of a better world.

Photo Credits: EFE / Walter Hupiú: 12; EFE / Felipe Trueba: 21; Natursports / Shutterstock.com: 1, 2, 8, 16, 25; Photo Works / Shutterstock.com: 4; Sportgraphic / Shutterstock.com: 18, 22, 26; Mutari / Wikimedia: 19.

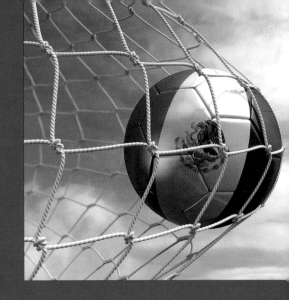

TABLE OF CONTENTS

Giovani Dos Santos controls the ball during a 2011 CONCACAF Gold Cup match at the Rose Bowl in Pasadena, California.

What a Goal!

Direct Pass to Brazil 2013

THEIR FACES COULD NOT LIE. The Mexican players were worried and dismayed. It was just twenty-three minutes into the final game of the 2011 CONCACAF Gold Cup and the United States team was already winning with two goals! The pressure was great—but the Mexican national team would not give up.

Striker Giovani dos Santos, a young man of Brazilian and Mexican heritage, had made things very clear in an interview just a few minutes before the game. "The past is behind ... either you are a champion or you fail," he told reporter Victor Casarrea.

The stadium was packed. Most of the 90,000 fans gathered at the Rose Bowl in Pasadena, California, on June 25, 2011, were supporters of the U.S. team. The United States was the host country and had organized the tournament. But this didn't discourage the Mexican players, who knew that they had to win. After several attempts, the goals started coming.

Pablo Barrera scored the first goal for the "Tri" in the 29th minute, which was followed by another by Andres Guardado in the 47th minute, one that he scored after Giovani crashed a ball on a defense. At halftime, the teams were tied. However, the Mexican national team would not settle for a draw—the Tri wanted to win.

Giovani Dos Santos was very active after returning from the break. In the 49th minute he sent the ball through the air and down to the right edge of the penalty area, but was rejected by the U.S. defense. The rebound was won by Andres Guardado. He took the ball and sent it to Pablo Barrera, who would again score a goal, Mexico's third of the game. Now it was the American players who were looking worried and feared they were losing their chance at victory.

With Mexico holding a 3-2 lead, the Tri seized on a chance to increase their advantage. Javier "Chicharito" Hernandez fought for the ball in the right side and passed it to Gerardo Torrado. As soon as he had it, Torrado passed it to Giovani. Dos Santos took the ball and came face to face with Tim Howard, the American goalkeeper. Watching Howard's hands, Gio concentrated on the play as if he had pictured scoring the goal in his mind. He kicked the ball with his fabulous left leg, almost without looking. The defenders couldn't do anything.

The ball spun in the air and went down, right between the crossbar and the upper left corner. The ball went inside through a place where nobody could reach it. That score—which would give the Mexican national team a resounding victory—would later be named be the "best goal" of the 2011 Gold Cup.

Thanks to Giovani Dos Santos, who with his talent, speed, and commitment once again captured the world's attention, Mexico earned a ticket for the FIFA Confederations Cup, which would be held in Brazil in 2013.

A Boy with Magic Legs

Giovani Dos Santos was born on May 11, 1989, in Mexico City, the capital of Mexico. But he grew up in Monterrey, an industrial city north of the country, which is said by soccer lovers to be the city with the most enthusiastic supporters.

His football ability comes from birth. His father, Gerardo Francisco dos Santos, better known as Zizinho, was born in

Despite being the son of a famous player like Zizinho, who played for Brazil and in several first division teams in Mexico, Gio's first opportunity to practice soccer was in a children's club, and came almost by chance. The little boy started playing at the age of six and stood out in each one of the seasons, in state and national events where he participated. He was the scoring champion for several years and at the age of 12 he had the chance to represent his country in France. From this event came one of the greatest opportunities of his career—to play in Spain.

Brazil. Like Giovani, he played for his national team as well as professionally in Mexico. Giovani's father played for Club America, Leon (which won the championship when Zizinho was with them), and Necaxa. He spent his last years playing for a Quick Soccer team called Monterrey La Raza. It was there, in the city of Monterrey, where Zizinho raised his family.

Gio, as Giovani Dos Santos is called, loved football since his early childhood, but his father wanted him and his two brothers, Jonathan and Eder, to focus more on studies. Giovani shared this memory in a Televisa Deportes broadcast titled "Life in Green." "It was not like my dad didn't want us to be football players, but as always, he said that studies came first," he said.

Undoubtedly, Zizinho has been a very important influence on Giovani's career. His father was a hero to Gio and his brother Jonathan, besides being their first teacher. He taught them the basics of football. Gio would later explain, "I think my father has been able to give us very good advice."

Despite having a strong influence from his dad, Gio started playing in a kids' club by accident. The opportunity came when he was only six years old. His parents were in Los Angeles, California, and a friend of the family's took Gio to a soccer camp where her son was training. The son was a friend of Gio's. When asked if he wanted to play too, Gio said yes. He was introduced to the coach, who put him in the midfield.

Fast Fact

Gio won the Top Scorer award for several years, when he was still a very young boy.

Gio was the star in his very first game. "That day we won by 10 to 2. I scored eight times and the coach was delighted," the player recalled.

Soccer Experience as a Little Boy

Giovani astonished those who met him. His talent was obvious. This would be disclosed by the coach of the youth team of CF Monterrey, Hector Becerra, in an ESPN broadcast. "I had the chance to meet Giovani, who had very important football attributes since he was very small," Becerra said. "He had a very good shot, very good beat, and a great technique."

After his debut in a children's club, Giovani played for Sao Paolo, a team that his father created and where his brother Jonathan played too. They were champions in four of the six league tournaments during 1997-2001. In the remaining two, they were runners-up. Giovani was the scoring champion in five of these tournaments and he was named Youth Sports Figure twice.

From 1998 to 2000, Dos Santos participated in several tournaments with Sao Paolo: the Chivas, Monterrey, Cruz

Barcelona FC's famous La Masia youth training facility, where Giovani began playing when he was eleven years old.

Azul and Dallas cups. He was the scoring champion in all of them. In 1999 and 2001 the team represented Nuevo Leon in two national tournaments, where Gio won the scoring title again.

Thanks to this last tournament, and now affiliated with the youth team of CF Monterrey, the Rayados, they were Mexico's representatives at the Danone Nations Cup, a tournament for 10-to-12 year olds held in France in 2001. That year, the second year of the Nations Cup, 24 teams participated. While in Europe, Giovani Dos Santos caught the attention of Catalan businessmen who would hire him to play in Spain.

Spain in Sight

GIOVANI DOS SANTOS WAS 12 YEARS OLD WHEN HE WENT TO France to represent Mexico in the Danone Nations Cup. His team finished fourth of 24 teams, and the young Mexican player shined as he had been playing for many years. Once again he was the event's scoring champion. His exploits were noticed by some Spanish businessmen, who wanted him to play in their country. No one in the dos Santos family could guess how radically their lives were about to change.

Signed in the Hallway

After the tournament, when they were back at their hotel, Giovani and his brother Jonathan were playing soccer in the lobby, as if it were a professional field. Their father was in a business meeting in one of the rooms.

Germán "Manny" Vaya Ballabriga, the man who recruited the brothers,

remembers that moment. "Well, it's funny, because I signed Gio in the hotel lobby," he recalled. "I was napping, and they [Jonathan and Giovani] kicked a ball into the hall and began playing in the hallway," he recalls.

The ball was flying from place to place and the kids were running and kicking, forgetting that it was not the place to play, when Ballabriga appeared.

They did not realize that he was a talent scout for FC Barcelona.

"I came out and said 'Hey, what's going on here?'" Ballabriga said during an ESPN special on Gio. "I saw the two brothers and told Gio, 'tell your dad to come, to go upstairs.' The kids said, 'No, please, we will stop.' But I insisted: 'No, Bring him up.'"

Former football player Gerardo dos Santos also recalls the meeting in the Paris hotel room. "We went and the man said, 'I like Giovani and Jonathan' and said that he was interested in taking them to Barcelona, and right there we began to talk."

It seemed like a practical joke, but that night the life of the dos Santos family would take a complete turn. Both Giovani and Jonathan were hired to play for the youth team of FC Barcelona, and so began Gio's historic rise.

Goodbye to Monterrey

Giovani was about to sign a contract to join CF Monterrey, but suddenly he was contemplating another life in a new continent, with new friends, a new team and a great future. "That's the way God wanted it, that I would be in Europe at 12," says Gio with a broad smile when asked why he left his country at such a small age. "Barcelona appeared and I didn't think twice," he adds.

The Rayados were upset to be losing this promising young player. The team even considered demanding money from Barça in exchange, because Gio supposedly had promised to sign the contract. However, CF Monterrey eventually agreed to let Gio go to Spain.

Today, the Monterrey club is honored to have had Giovani in their youth system, even for a short time. The president of CF Monterrey, Jorge Urdiales, once said to reporters about Giovani: "It's pride of origin, to know that he came from Monterrey, that he is a Regio, that he was

Giovani was the scoring champion when he went to France to represent Mexico. This caught the scouts' attention, who saw the children (Giovani and Jonathan) playing football in the hotel corridors. They asked them to call their father so they could talk to him. The boys thought that they would be rebuked. They didn't suspect that at that very moment they would be made an offer that would change their lives.

The boys' father signed a contract for them with the Youth Divisions of FC Barcelona. Gio would eventually be the scoring champion for the Barça junior team in several seasons. His great skills on the soccer field caught the eye of coaches with the Barça senior team as well as his own country's U-17 national team.

raised by his father's good hand in a local amateur team, and later with us, in the basic forces."

The Conquest of Spain

In 2002 Giovani arrived in Spain to play for the youth team of FC Barcelona. He had also a heavy weight on his back, as those who were near him at that time say.

"So he arrived as a cadet and I remember this: that volatility, that speed, that agility, that strength; such great attributes that he still posseses. And even more, importantly in those times when I had kids who had not made the switch from boy to man yet. Well, that's what he faced and much more," recalled Albert Benaijes, Barcelona Football Base Coordinator.

Meanwhile Sergio Lobero, Gio's coach in Juvens of Barcelona, thinks that the young man had to pass through a lot of hard changes.

"He was at a very early age when he joined in. He was a very young player, and sometimes those situations surpass you a little. The fact of coming to a club as important as Barcelona, but also to a new country, a new city, a new culture."

Fast Fact

Giovani and Jonathan dos Santos impressed Catalan entrepreneurs who signed them to play in Spain. The contract was signed at the same hotel where they were staying.

The FC Barcelona youth team was league champions in 2004-2005 and 2005-2006. Gio was the scoring champion in the 2002-2003, 2003-2004, and 2004-2005 seasons. His technique was impeccable and his attributes were hard to ignore. His speed, courage, and strength led to a lot of goals.

His achievments attracted much attention, especially from soccer coaches in Mexico. They would soon ask Gio to take off the jersey of FC Barcelona and put on the colors of Mexico. Once he did that, the whole world would be watching.

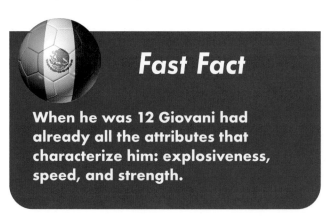

Fast Fact

When he was 12 Giovani had already all the attributes that characterize him: explosiveness, speed, and strength.

Gio fights for the ball with Vurnon Anita during Mexico's semifinal match against the Netherlands during the FIFA U-17 World Cup tournament. Mexico would go on to defeat favored Brazil and win its first U-17 title.

Giovani Leaps to Fame

OPPORTUNITY KNOCKED FOR GIOVANI DOS SANTOS. In the spring of 2005, he was invited to represent his country in a World Cup event. The Mexican Football Federation (FMF) summoned him to play for its under-17 team in the FIFA U-17 World Championship, to be held in Peru. Gio had not appeared in an international event like this since he was 12. Now he could show the world how much his football skills had improved in Spain.

Gio agreed to join the team, but he first had to fulfill some commitments with his youth team in Spain. When he finally joined the Mexican under-17 team, there was only a week before the knockout stage began. Upon arrival, Giovani played three games as a substitution, helping his team with two goals. Mexico qualified for the finals.

It was the moment of truth and this time Giovani was summoned to be a regular player. And although the coach,

Jesus Ramirez, placed him in a slightly more forward position than Gio was used to playing, the young man shone from the beginning. Gio caused a sensation with two assists that gave the U-17 squad a win over Uruguay.

The Mexican national team moved on to the next round, facing Costa Rica in the quarterfinals. Mexico won this match with daring and courage. During the next semifinal game, against the Netherlands, Gio would once again

Fast Fact

The outstanding work of Giovani dos Santos at the U-17 World Cup, assisting on many scoring plays, earned him the Silver Ball.

provide two assists. Those two passes would be engraved in the fans' minds as Mexico won, 4-0.

Now in the final, Mexico was going to face the Brazilian team. The youth team from Gio's father's country was considered the tournament favorite by most people. But this did not intimidate Gio and his teammates. From Gio's skillful moves that overpowered two Brazilian players came a play that Carlos Vela turned into a goal at the 31st minute. A minute later, Omar Esparza would score Mexico's second goal. When the game ended, the Tri had a 3-0 victory and Mexico had won the U-17 championship.

Giovani won the silver ball as the second-best player of the tournament, only behind Anderson, the Brazilian player. After that tournament, nothing would be the same for Gio.

Giomania

The national fervor cascaded on the boys of the U-17 team, who had won the first FIFA World Cup for Mexico ever. The wide advantage over Brazil in the final score made them invincible in the eyes of the fans. Gio's popularity, like that of his companions, was through the roof.

"I was 17. All down the street everyone knew my name. Everybody had heard of me. They shouted 'Mexico!' We were on the bus and the cars stopped in the street," remembers Gio about what they experienced after the tournament.

The kids became national heroes. And if this were not enough, fame was chasing Giovani. It was not a Mexican club but FC Barcelona that would open the doors for him; Barcelona signed him when he was still a minor. So began Gio's story with the big boys.

His time with Barça

Giovani was called up by FC Barcelona in the 2006-2007 preseason. The young prospect had a spectacular debut, scoring for the club in his first game. But despite his efforts to win a place in the first team, the board decided that Gio was not ready yet.

It was not until the following season, when the young man had acquired Spanish citizenship and was 18, that he could join Barça completely, being the main scorer in the pre-season games.

Gio scored five goals, including a very important one in the team's game at the Joan Gamper Cup tournament. He later recalled, "It was a dream debut against Inter. To tell the truth, I did not believe myself. I debuted, I kicked a penalty shot and scored."

Giovani exceeded all expectations.

Although he said that he would probably not participate much in the first season, he was active in 28 games and recorded 8 assists. In addition he kicked two penalty shots and scored three goals.

But during the season Barça did not see the results that it expected and unfortunately Gio's performance was affected.

Again in the Green Shirt

Giovani was still with Barça in 2007 when Mexican coach Chucho Ramirez called him to play for Mexico in a World Cup. This time he would play with the U-20 team. The manager, trying to have most of the U-17 champions in the team, summoned them all although some were younger than their rivals.

They did fine in the pre-qualifying round. Gio scored three goals that sent the team to the FIFA U-20 World Cup to be held in Canada. Giovani was brilliant in the first game, scoring a goal that would later be voted the second-best of the tournament. Then in the game that they played against Portugal, Gio was granted a penalty kick: after a breakaway of the

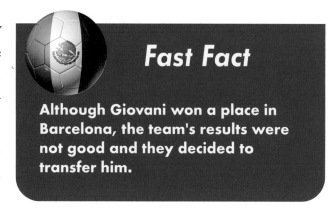

Fast Fact

Although Giovani won a place in Barcelona, the team's results were not good and they decided to transfer him.

Mexican team, despair had seized the Portuguese players and had committed a foul. Gio turned this violation into a goal.

In the second round the Mexican U-20 team won the game against Congo. In this match Giovani dos Santos scored his third goal of the tournament. However, the Mexican U-20 team did not duplicate the success of the U-17 team a few years earlier. In the game against Argentina—the team that would later win the Cup—Mexico lost 1-0 and had to return home without success.

Still, Giovani did not return empty-handed. He received the Bronze Ball for his goals in the tournament and he was also called the third most valuable player in the competition.

Gio was thrilled when he was summoned by the Tri to play a friendly match against Panama in September 2007.

Chapter
4

The Burden of Fame

GIOVANI DOS SANTOS HAD ADVANCED QUICKLY since childhood. Virtually without seeking them, opportunities had come knocking on the young Mexican's door. He had accomplished much thanks to his natural talent for dribbling the ball, but also his determination against rivals, speed, courage, strength, and awesome left leg. These were his main credentials. That's why so much was expected from him. Very soon, comparisons began.

Distressing Comparisons

In Mexico and the world, Giovani was seen as the next big star of international football. After Mexico's triumph at the U-17 World Cup and his successful debut in a first division Spanish team, many saw him as the natural successor to Mexican soccer star Cuauhtemoc Blanco. But Gio just wanted to be himself.

"I would like to become a reference, and to be what Cuauhtemoc Blanco has been for my country. But I want to live my own story," said Gio. In this regard, Quique Wolf, sports commentator for ESPN, said that it was not good to put

Giovani dos Santos's fame led to comparisions with soccer greats like Cuauhtemoc Blanco, Ronaldhino, and Lionel Messi that would prove to be a heavy burden on him.

so much pressure on Giovani, or treat him as the successor to Cuauhtemoc Blanco. "What he has to do," the reporter said, "is to be Giovani dos Santos."

However, this was not the only comparison that was made between Giovani and other players. He was also compared to the world famous Ronaldinho, his Brazilian teammate in Barcelona. It was a great satisfaction for Giovani to be told that he had characteristics similar to Ronaldinho, but it was also a lot of pressure since he was only 16.

"Ronaldinho is Ronaldinho, and I hope to make my own story," said Giovani. His partner and friend Ronaldinho always expressed himself favorably about Gio in TV interviews, saying that to some extent comparisons were to be expected, because they both were forwards. "I think that we play pretty much the same position and we are attackers, forwards and I think what we like is to dribble and make plays. We're a lot alike," said the Brazilian soccer star.

Gio also was compared to Lionel Messi, the Argentine soccer star, who was considered to be the best player in the world.

Javier Aguirre, the coach of the Mexican team, believed that those comparisons were hurting Gio. Luck was not on the Mexican's side. Despite teammate Ronaldinho's kind words about Gio, FC Barcelona fans and directors came to feel that Gio didn't deliver on his promise. The young man could not live up to the high expectations that everyone had.

After the 2007-08 season ended, Barça sold Gio to Tottenham Hotspur, a first division club in England. The transfer fee was 6 million Euros.

In English Soccer

Gio's arrival was a highly anticipated one and Tottenham was happy with its new purchase, as they dedicated to the cover of its official magazine to Gio. The move also seemed to please Gio at the beginning.

With Tottenham Gio was reunited with Juan de Ramos, who had been his coach at Barcelona. However, the 2008-09 season did not go as well as he had hoped it would. The coach was fired due to the team's poor results and Gio suffered an ankle injury.

The international press was very hard on him, and it was common to read headlines like, "Gio's Humiliating Decline."

When new manager Harry Redknapp arrived, Gio was relegated to the bench. He played just 12 games for Tottenham, then was loaned to a second-division team, Ipswich Town. They were hard times.

"In the beginning it was a bit tricky. Just imagine: Barcelona, Tottenham, then Ipswich? I still don't know what was going through my head in that moment, honestly," he said to a reporter who asked him about his little participation in the season.

Those were not easy times, although Giovani played well for Ipswich Town,

Giovani played his first match for Barça in July 2006, scoring against Danish club AGF Aarhus.

scoring four goals in eight games. He went back to Tottenham Hotspur before the start of the 2009-10 season.

As if this were not enough, other incidents marked him and not necessarily for good.

Fall from Grace

Despite all the high hopes about Gio's arrival at Tottenham Hotspur, things did not go quite right for Gio, who began to show a lack of discipline both on and off the field. He fell in with a bad crowd and began staying out late, partying and drinking. This affected his game, making him less successful on the field.

While in 2008 he had been ranked among the 100 most talented young football players by *Don Balón* magazine, at the end of the year the British press published some photographs showing a drunk and sleepless Giovani. These distressing pictures appeared around the world. They harmed his career, because the club's directors didn't like his attitude and continued leaving him on the bench.

In addition, in 2009 Giovani became very distracted as he started a new romantic relationship that was featured in every gossip magazine. His girlfriend was Belinda, a pop singer from Monterrey, and he began to suffer the harassment of the press. Now Giovani was appearing more in gossip magazines than in sport journals. Even *People* magazine in Spanish fatured the young Mexican as one of the most handsome players in the world. While his Romeo fame increased, he gave little to talk about in the field.

Although Gio recorded an assist in his first game of 2009-10, he soon suffered an ankle injury in a game against Preston North End. It took time for him to recover, and he missed most of the season as a

Giovani dos Santos's fame began to grow after his triumph with the Mexican U-17 team, as well as his successes with the basic forces of Barcelona. However, as he became famous he was sometimes compared to outstanding Mexican and international players. Some considered him to be the successor to the great Mexican Cuauhtemoc Blanco; others believed he would be the "next" Ronaldinho. Gio was even compared to Lionel Messi, considered to be the best player in the world. Giovani said he was only working to be himself.

The comparisons led fans and sports experts to expect too much from him. As if this were not enough pressure, Giovani started to go out with the wrong crowd and began to stay up late and drink alcohol. He also had a highly publicized romance with Belinda, a singer from Monterrey, Mexico. Giovani started to be featured in gossip magazines, while appearing less and less on sports news.

Giovani dos Santos fight for the ball with the Korean Hwang Seok-Ho during their match at the London Olympic Games in 2012.

result. Even when he was healthy, his coaches did not let him play much. It was a frustrating time for the young player.

One good thing that occurred during that time was when Giovani was summoned to play in the senior Mexican national team, a dream come true, as childhood friend Gustavo Nuño remembered in an ESPN broadcast.

"I remember that he told me that his dream was to play for the national team. And he used to say that his favorite Mexican team was Club America, and that someday he would like to play there. But first of all, of course, his dream was to be in the Mexican team."

Fast Fact

Giovani started going out with a bad crowd. He stayed up late, going to clubs to drink and meet women. This distracted him from his athletic career.

Chapter 5

Giovani dos Santos celebrates after scoring a goal for Racing de Santander in a Spanish League match, April 2011. He was on loan from Tottenham.

A Dream Come True

DESPITE THE DIFFICULT SITUATION THAT Giovani dos Santos was experiencing in Europe, a few good things would present themselves. The best was an invitation to join the senior national team to represent his country again. Giovani debuted with the "Tri" on September 9, 2007. Starting in 2008 he began to play in pre-qualifying matches for the World Cup.

His performances began to be noticed in mid-2009, when he found the goal again and scored twice against Venezuela during a friendly match. As he continued playing, Gio's game improved dramatically and his participation in the 2009 CONCACAF Gold Cup earned him the MVP award, having scored three goals. Mexican coach Javier Aguirre included Gio in the team that would travel to South Africa in 2010 to fight for the World Cup.

Meanwhile, thanks to his recent achievements in the Gold Cup, several job offers arrived, but they did not materialize. Giovani was being courted by several European teams, including Deportivo La Coruña in Spain, Inter Milan, Olympiacos of Greece, and Paris Saint-Germain. Redknapp, the coach at Tottenham, promised Gio that he would get more playing time. However, the coach did not fulfill his promise to get Gio on the field more.

After a landslide victory by 5 to 0 against Doncaster Rovers, Gio returned to the bench. Feeling very frustrated, he decided to take an offer to join Galatasaray of Turkey for the rest of the 2009-10 season. He wanted more playing time, so that he would be physically prepared to participate in the World Cup in South Africa.

Great Reception

The welcome for Giovani dos Santos at the airport in Turkey was truly impressive. He was there to join the Galatasaray team on loan from Tottenham Hotspur. The displays of affection from fans greatly encouraged the Mexican player.

"The reception was awesome," Gio told the press. "I did not expect this. I think I was stunned on arrival. It was something I had never had, a reception of this size. I am very happy and I promise to work very hard. Obviously this is a motivation, a challenge, to see that the fans are here to support me. A challenge to do well in the field, right?"

Success and Slips

The promising soccer star wanted to do well again and show what he was made of. His national team's performance in the World Cup in South Africa had not been very good; they had returned empty-handed after being eliminated by Argentina in the second round. Giovani didn't score, but was still distinguished as the second best young player of the tournament.

In 2011, Giovani was called again to participate in Copa America with the national team, but they were eliminated and passed through a major scandal of indiscipline and lack of morals. Eight players were punished for it and this affected the team. When the Mexican team

Giovani dos Santos has had successes and failures in his career. Actually, not everything has been his fault. One example was Mexico's poor showing in the 2011 Copa America. The scandal in which eight players were involved, and their resulting punishment, made the team weak on the field.

Unfortunately, Tottenham Hotspur managers still do not trust him. On several occasions they have transfered Gio to other teams. Some of these teams have been considerably worse than the English club—teams like Santander that have almost gone down to a lesser division, but thanks to Giovani they managed to stay in first division. However, when the loan ended, Giovani went back to Tottenham, where they neither sell him nor let him play. If Giovani wants to end his struggles, he will have to return to the path of discipline. Hard work and focus on soccer will help him to make it out of this difficult stretch that he is currently in.

Gio played for the Tricolor in the 2011 Copa America, but Mexico did not perform well.

was sent home, Giovani was asked about the team's poor performance. He replied, "We all knew how hard this was going to be, after all the problems outside the sports field. Whether you want it or not, they affected the team's performance.

"My summer has not been fully bad," he added. "I won a championship and to tell the truth, I'm happy."

And it was true, Giovani had had an excellent performance in the 2011 Gold Cup, where he scored two goals against Cuba in the qualifiers, and was fortunate enough to score that fantastic goal that eliminated the United States in the final, the one distinguished as the best goal in the tournament.

Still at Tottenham

In half a season with Galatasaray Gio did not score, although he did make several assists. Gio returned to Tottenham in the summer of 2010, and spent the rest of the year with the English club.

In January 2011 Giovani was sent out again, this time to the Spanish League club Racing Santander on loan. Racing even spoke about the possibility of purchasing his services from Tottenham. Gio's performance with this team was very

Giovani is still at Tottenham Hotspur. He has not been allowed to go forth to seek new horizons, but the club has not let him play much on the field either.

important. The young man scored his first goal for Racing in a match played on February 27, 2011, against Villareal. His performance throughout the season was very good, and he got his first double in the Spanish first division in a 3-2 win over Hércules CF. That victory helped Racing stay in the premier league and avoid relegation to the second division, as the club had feared.

Giovani had to leave the team at the end of the 2010-11 season and return to Tottenham Hotspur. It seems he will stay at Tottenham for now. The young player has had offers from several Spanish clubs, including Sevilla, Granada, Racing Santander, and Villarreal, and has even drawn interest from Portuguese, American, and Russian teams. However, there has been no agreement to move.

The English team's position regarding Giovani has seemed strange to many observers. While keeping him on the bench and not letting him play, the team has also avoided a possible sale to another club. On January 30, 2012, the Spanish newspaper *Superdeporte* ("Super Sport") reported on the status of the young Mexican player: "When his arrival at Villareal seemed a fact, Tottenham changed its position and decided to stop the Mexican transfer in either direction. The negotiation has been locked, and unless the English club

Fast Fact

Giovani Dos Santos's career has fallen into some bumps, but with the championship at the 2011 Gold Cup, he hopes to take once more the place that he had in Mexican and international football.

changes its position, the attacker will not leave London."

Struggling to Overcome

The last years in Giovani dos Santos's career have not been easy. The team that hired him hasn't let him play much. But some of this is due to his lack of discipline. Therefore, the power to change this situation is in Giovani's hands. If he can focus on soccer and develop his talents, perhaps he can win back the trust of the management at Tottenham.

Gio summarized his feelings in one of the many interviews about his footballing career: "I have only good experiences. Even the bad times have helped me to mature." Now, new horizons are in front of him. His contract with Tottenham expires in 2013. That year, he may once again excite Mexican fans with a top performance in the Confederations Cup in Brazil.

GLOSSARY

assist—when a player passes the ball to another player and that player finishes the play by scoring.

ball possession—action or effect of having the ball, keeping the other team from controlling it.

coach—professional in charge of developing and organizing a team's strategy.

Champions League—the most important international soccer tournament in Europe.

CONCACAF—the Confederation Cup in North, Central American and Caribbean Confederation is the international football association that includes countries from North America, Central America, the Caribbean islands, and the South American countries of Guyana, Suriname, and French Guiana. CONCACAF is one of the six FIFA confederations. Copa Libertadores de América—the most important soccer tournament in the Americas.

counterattack—strategy that consists of making the most of the other team's lack of organization after it has just attacked.

defender—a player who helps to protect the goal area and blocks attacks by the opponent. Within the defense there are various positions: central defender, side defender, and free defender.

extra time—playing time added to the end of a soccer match to make up for lost time caused by interruptions during the match due to fouls, injuries, or warnings.

forward—the player whose mission it is to "attack" (move the ball forward against) the opposite team.

fútbol Sala (futsal)—a game like soccer that is played in a smaller area (often indoors and on a cement floor), with fewer players. It is also known as fútbol de salón or microfutbol.

GLOSSARY

goalkeeper—player in charge of the goal; he is the only one allowed to use his hands in the game.

group stage—stage in the World Cup competition where teams play a short tournament in which the top teams qualify to advance to the knockout round.

jersey—sports clothing that covers the player's upper body and serves to identify the team for which he plays.

knockout round—stage in certain competitions where the team that loses a match is out of the entire competition.

midfielder—player in charge of building up the attack from the middle of the field.

referee—a judge in charge of making sure the rules of the game are followed, and who settles conflicts.

soccer—the term used to describe European football in the United States.

striker—a soccer team's top-scoring forward who usually plays around the center of the team's forwards.

tactics—the strategic plan and soccer philosophy that a coach chooses to employ, after studying the strategies of an opposing team.

World Cup—most important soccer competition in the world, organized by FIFA.

FURTHER READING

Perez Ferreiro, Sebastian. "The Bad News: Gio Not Taking Off in Europe," *Sports Illustrated Latino* (May 30, 2010).

Reyes Diaz, Abel. "2011 A Good Year for the Tricolor," *ESPN Magazine* (December 2011).

Ramirez, Carlos F. *Eleven Decades of Mexican Soccer.* Mexico: Editorial Octavio Antonio Colmenares and Vargas, 2010.

Lucht, Roman. *The Football Life.* Argentina, Editorial Sudamericana, 2011.

INTERNET RESOURCES

http://www.tottenhamhotspur.com

The official website of Tottenham, the English team where Giovani Dos Santos currently plays.

http://www.giodosantos.com

The official website of Giovani Dos Santos.

http://www.fifa.com

Official site of FIFA (Federation Internationale de Football Association).

http://www.concacaf.com

Official Website of CONCACAF, the international football association that includes countries in North America, Central America, the Caribbean islands, and the South American countries of Guyana, Suriname, and French Guiana. CONCACAF is one of the six FIFA confederations.

http://www.femexfut.org.mx

Website of the Mexican Soccer Federation, the organization responsible for governing futbol in Mexico.

INDEX